THE FAMOUS GROUSE

A WHISKY COMPANION

THE
FAMOUS
GROUSE

A WHISKY
COMPANION

Heritage, History, Recipes & Drinks

10 9 8 7 6 5 4 3

Published in 2011 by Ebury Press, an imprint of Ebury Publishing

A Random House Group Company

Copyright © The Famous Grouse 2011

The Famous Grouse has asserted its right to be identified as the author of this Work in accordance with the Copyright, Designs and Patents Act 1988

The Random House Group Limited Reg. No. 954009
Addresses for companies within the Random House Group can be found at www.randomhouse.co.uk

A CIP catalogue record for this book is available from the British Library

The Random House Group Limited supports The Forest Stewardship Council®(FSC®), the leading international forest certification organisation. Our books carrying the FSC label are printed on FSC® certified paper. FSC is the only forest certification scheme endorsed by the leading environmental organisations, including Greenpeace. Our paper procurement policy can be found at www.randomhouse.co.uk/environment

To buy books by your favourite authors and register for offers visit www.randomhouse.co.uk

Design by Turnbull Grey www.turnbullgrey.co.uk

Illustration by Martin Haake

Printed and bound in China by C & C Offset Printing Co., Ltd

ISBN 9780091944742

CONTENTS

THE
FAMOUS
GROUSE

HERITAGE

IN THE BEGINNING

The principles of distilling have long been understood. Alcohol boils at a lower temperature than water so, if you collect a quantity of a low-strength alcohol in a closed vessel and heat it gently at around 80°C, the vapour that comes off first will be predominantly alcohol. Collect and condense that vapour and you will have a distilled spirit. Repeat the process until a satisfactory strength is reached and – *voilà* – you have invented distilling. Or, rather, re-invented it, as these basic principles have been understood since at least the 11th century and probably earlier.

If you start with wine, the eventual end product will be brandy; start with a beer-like liquid and what you get is the raw material for whisky. But, please, don't try this at home.

In fact, the first recorded distilling was done by alchemists who were trying to turn base metal into gold and were fascinated by the transformative nature of the distilling process, and by herbalists, physicians and monks who were preparing early medicines. Medieval texts on distilling abound, with early science and mysticism intermingled.

So it's no surprise that the first written mention of whisky in Scotland dates from June 1494 and involves one Friar John Cor of Lindores Abbey in Fife. This was founded around 1190 by David, Earl of Huntingdon for Tironensian monks and was one of the most important of Scotland's religious settlements. Sadly, the abbey was sacked by a mob from Dundee in 1543 and again by John Knox and his supporters in 1559. Today, all that remains is a few ruins scattered within a farm. But it is still whisky's spiritual home, and its place in whisky's history will never be forgotten. Friar Cor paid duty on 'eight Bols of malt wherewith to make Aqua Vitae'; enough to make him about 1,500 bottles of whisky – which suggests that it wasn't the first time someone had fired up a still.

From the end of the 15th century for the next 300 years there isn't a lot to report. Distilling in Scotland was undertaken on a small scale in great houses and on farms for immediate, local consumption. In fact, we probably wouldn't recognize the spirit made back then as whisky, certainly not as we know it today. It would have been quite harsh, probably strongly flavoured with spices or fruit to make it more palatable and unlikely to have been aged for any length of time.

For small farmers though, whisky was the ideal product: it converted a high-volume, low-value cereal crop into a high-value, low-volume product that was easy to store and to transport using ponies or a simple cart. Many farmers used it to pay their workers, or even their rent. Illicit distilling also flourished.

THE ARRIVAL OF BLENDING

By the late 1700s though, a recognizable industry was beginning to emerge and the distinction between Highland and Lowland whisky was quite marked. Highland whisky was a more artisanal product, produced in small pot stills and generally preferred

for its quality; Lowland whisky was distilled quickly on an impressively industrial scale, but much of it was destined for London, where it was re-distilled and flavoured with juniper to be sold as gin. Robert Burns was not impressed with the Lowland whisky of the day – he called it 'a most rascally liquor'.

But the early Lowland distillers pioneered a form of continuous still, which allowed them to produce whisky quickly and cheaply, and by 1830 this had been developed into what became known as a 'Coffey Still', after its inventor Aeneas Coffey, an Irish former excise officer and distiller. Fortunately for Scotland, his countrymen turned their back on this innovation, leaving the field clear for the Scots distillers.

The significance of the continuous still was that it permitted blending – put simply, mixing the more strongly flavoured Highland single malts with a quantity of the grain whisky from the continuous still. Because this was both more delicate and available in larger quantities, it became possible to mix, or blend, the two types together to provide a highly palatable, affordable and easy-to-drink product that rapidly found favour with drinkers the world over. Blended whisky hasn't looked back since.

WORLDWIDE SUCCESS

Several factors combined from the middle of the 19th century to assist Scotch whisky's rise to global prominence.

Firstly, the creation of blended whiskies ensured a consistent and reliable product that lent itself to the development of branding, a discipline that was just getting into its stride at this time (interestingly, the world's first trademark, issued in 1876, was for alcohol – the red triangle of Bass Pale Ale). We shall learn more about the importance of brands to Scotch whisky shortly.

Secondly, Scotland became very fashionable in Victorian Britain. The novels and poems of Sir Walter Scott; the paintings of Sir Edwin Henry Landseer; the advent of tourism (helped by the development of the railway network) and the influence of the Royal family in visiting Scotland all played a part here. Remarkably, George IV made the first visit of a reigning monarch to Scotland since 1650 in 1822, an event orchestrated by Scott with all the skill and ingenuity of a 21st-century spin doctor, and was seen to consume whisky (and not inconsiderable quantities of cherry brandy) with evident enjoyment. Enlightened legislation in 1822 and 1823 laid the foundations for the modern industry.

Royal visits by Queen Victoria and Prince Albert, their enthusiastic adoption of Scotland as a holiday destination and, in particular, their construction of Balmoral Castle from 1853 further enhanced Scotland's fashionable appeal. The patriotism of Scottish regiments in the service of the British crown only served to widen this favourable image.

Thirdly, at much the same time, brandy production was in severe decline due to the infestation of first French and then European vineyards by the phylloxera aphid, which destroyed the vines. No vines meant no grapes, which meant no wine could be produced and, in turn, no brandy could be distilled. Up to this point, broadly speaking, brandy had been the favoured spirit amongst refined drinkers, with whisky being seen as the drink of the working man and the rural poor. The shortage of brandy and the increased accessibility of blended Scotch changed this image for good.

Finally, the spread of the British Empire, often accompanied by Scottish troops, administrators and traders, ensured a global demand for whisky (and gin). It was patriotic to drink products from home, rather than adopt the local moonshine (though doubtless the latter served *in extremis*).

FROM MODEST BEGINNINGS

Based on these four factors, the great blending houses – founded by the forefathers of the so-called 'whisky barons' – were established. These were, for the most part, small local businesses, originally licensed grocers or wine and spirit merchants. Names such as Walker, Buchanan, Teacher and Haig reflect these origins.

Left to right:

MATTHEW GLOAG — 1814–1860
WILLIAM B. GLOAG — 1860–1896
MATTHEW GLOAG — 1896–1910
MATTHEW W. GLOAG 1910–1947

In the city of Perth, around 40 miles north of Edinburgh, several such firms were established. In 1825, Thomas Sandeman (of the famous port family) established a small shop in Perth, trading as a whisky merchant. He was joined by Arthur Bell, who, by the late 1840s, had become sole partner. John Dewar set up his business in 1843, but before them all came the first Matthew Gloag, who opened his shop in 1800. Today, Bells and Dewars are part of multinational corporations, with headquarters far from Perth and their local connections no more than history – but with offices in Perth, and the nearby Glenturret distillery, the Perth roots of Matthew Gloag & Son and The Famous Grouse remain to the fore.

Matthew Gloag traded in a modest way from 24 Atholl Street, Perth, for many years. His humble licensed grocer's shop served a burgeoning local trade, but his early training as butler and cellarman at Scone Palace stood him in good stead.

Once the crowning place of the kings of Scots, Scone Palace occupies a unique position in the history of Scotland. A breathtakingly beautiful place of power and mystery and the rightful home of the celebrated Stone of Destiny, Scone Palace is regarded as a national treasure. Today, the palace is home of the Earls of Mansfield, and a five-star visitor attraction to visitors from around the world, but in 1842 it was a luxurious private home for Mansfield's aristocratic ancestors.

In September 1842, two and a half years after her marriage, Queen Victoria visited Scone with Prince Albert on their way through the Highlands (a trip that led to their love of Scotland). The preparations for the royal visit included the commission of a grand dining table, which is still used for formal occasions today, and Matthew Gloag was invited to supply the catering for the impressive banquet held to mark the Queen's visit. Fortunately, everything seemed to go well, one observer remarking of Gloag's provisions, 'The fruits, confection, etc., were such as to do him general credit in the selection.'

His business went from strength to strength, and in 1870 he was succeeded by his son William, a wine connoisseur, shrewd businessman and a man who keenly appreciated quality in whisky. At a time when it was still associated with rough Highlanders, he described it as an 'exhilarating drink ... invaluable in restoring the exhausted forces of nature.'

He also understood the importance of using the finest ingredients and careful maturation in high quality sherry casks. In the 1870s he wrote:

> *It is of paramount importance that only the very best materials that can be procured should be used in the manufacture of whisky. When these only are used and when the whisky has been sufficiently matured in sherry casks (which are of unpurchasable benefit to it), there can be no more wholesome spirit, and in purity, fragrance and ease of digestion it is superior to the finest French brandy.*

In this he was ahead of many of his contemporaries, though great businesses were being created by his local rivals Bells and Dewars and by other progressive Scots blenders and distillers. This was a vibrant and exciting period for Scotch whisky, which led to a great boom in production and the building of many new distilleries.

Though it had been founded in 1798, Highland Park distillery on Orkney doubled in size in 1898 and The Macallan, on Speyside, was also significantly improved and enlarged in the 1890s. Nearby Glenrothes was built in 1878 and in 1887 formed part of the original Highland Distilleries Ltd. All three of these fine single malt whiskies are to this day a critical part of The Famous Grouse blend and in the ownership of the successor company Highland Distillers.

THE GROUSE TAKES FLIGHT

By now, Scotland's Victorian fashionability was at its peak. Wealthy aristocrats built or expanded their Highland sporting estates, and successful entrepreneurs and businessmen copied them. The railway had come to Perth with the opening of Sir William Tite's splendid station in 1847–8. At one time, nine platforms served the busy connections establishing Perth as a major gateway to the Highlands and there was much excellent sport to be had around Perth, either salmon fishing in the River Tay or grouse shooting on the nearby hills.

Local businesses, such as hotels, outfitters, sporting goods shops and wine and spirit merchants naturally benefitted, Matthew Gloag & Son amongst them. In 1896, William's nephew Matthew returned from a long period working in the Bordeaux wine trade and took over the firm. At that time, as befits a merchant and blender (the firm had no distilleries at this stage), many different whiskies were bottled, some 'single whiskies' (single malts as we would call them today) and some proprietary blends. One such was

Gloag's Perth Whisky, the firm then following the prevailing convention of using the principal's name.

The handsome red and black label featured an illustration of the graceful Smeaton's Bridge (completed in October 1771) over the River Tay and St Matthew's Church of Scotland with its dramatic 64.6 m (212 ft) spire, both important Perth landmarks.

No doubt it was popular, but Matthew was shortly to surpass its success with what proved to be his masterstroke, launching 'Grouse' whisky in 1896. The appeal to the sporting fraternity was immediately obvious and, instead of limiting his whisky by association with a business that was still essentially a provincial concern, he shrewdly employed a symbol that could stand for all of Scotland. It was a tactic that was to stand the test of time.

The following year his daughter Philippa drew the first red grouse to appear on the label and a whisky legend was born (or took flight, as one might say).

Like his father, Matthew celebrated and enjoyed great whisky, intuitively appreciating its importance to his countrymen. In 1896 he wrote of whisky:

Scotsmen the world over use it neat to warm them when cold, diluted to refresh them when warm, to revive them when exhausted, as a medicine in sickness, as an aid to digestion, as a sedative for sleeplessness, and, universally to celebrate the meeting with, or parting with, friends, confident that used in moderation it will suit the occasion as nothing else will do, and with nothing but good effect. Millions of men in every clime have found that these Scotsmen are right.

With his emphasis on moderation Matthew Gloag sounds almost our contemporary, though we might be able to tell him that – happily – millions of women have now joined their men folk in appreciating the conviviality associated with Scotch whisky.

1896 was not, however, the most fortuitous time to launch a new whisky, as the great Victorian whisky boom was about to come to an untimely end.

A Leith firm of blenders, Pattisons Ltd, had been engaged in much speculative trading and stock manipulation. In December 1898 the firm failed and, in a spectacular collapse, dragged nine other companies and many small suppliers with it. A criminal trial followed (the two Pattison brothers were jailed for fraud) but the damage had been done. Confidence was lost and the widespread realization that excessive stocks of whisky had been built up on easy credit led to a general depression in the Scotch whisky trade. There was also some loss of public confidence in blended whisky and the start of a long-running debate about the relative merits of blended versus single whisky that eventually led to the celebrated 'What is Whisky?' case and a subsequent Royal Commission.

So these were difficult and trying times, made worse by a general economic depression. But Matthew Gloag soldiered quietly on, his careful and methodical way of business being the saviour of the firm. 'Grouse' whisky grew slowly in the public's estimation, building a loyal following in Scotland and amongst discerning sportsmen, who would take the taste for this remarkable blend back home to England and, on occasion, further afield.

HAPPY BIRTHDAY

For the dedicated sportsman, one date assumes a significance above all others. That, of course, is 12 August, the so-called 'Glorious Twelfth', which since the Game Act of 1831 has marked the opening of the shooting season for red grouse (participants have until 10 December to fill their bags, after which the birds are safe for another nine months). The date has a greater significance to our story however, for it was on 12 August 1905 that Matthew Gloag, recognizing the growing popularity of his 'Grouse' brand, renamed it 'The Famous Grouse'.

The story goes that he re-registered the trademark as The Famous Grouse at the stroke of midnight on 12 August, though one might wonder how he

managed to persuade the civil servants to open their office at such an hour! There was certainly no online registration in those days – perish the thought that a bottle of whisky may have lubricated the hallowed doors. Whatever the circumstances, The Famous Grouse was now officially recognized and its birth date recorded for posterity.

From 1905 the firm carried on in family hands, expanding, developing its brands and spreading the fame of The Famous Grouse. By the 1920s whisky had overtaken wine as the principal part of the business. Despite the restrictions of Prohibition in the USA, by 1936 it was necessary to open a huge new warehouse and bottling line to supplement the considerable cellars at the Perth head office, Bordeaux House. Again this proved a sound move, as the stocks of whisky carried at the outbreak of World War II were anticipated to last for a dozen years or more, carrying the firm through a period of shortages as distilling was suspended during the war.

Since the 1920s the Scotch whisky industry has gone through a rollercoaster of boom and bust, resulting in many consolidations and mergers. One by one, smaller family firms were acquired by larger groups, some willingly, some as the result of hostile takeover, and the large multinational corporations that so dominate the global spirits market that we see today started to come into existence. The control of Scotch whisky started to drift out of Scotland, slowly at first then ever faster.

On the high streets of Scotland (and, indeed, across the whole of Britain) the traditional licensed grocer found it harder and harder to compete against the power of the supermarkets, and the face of traditional

THE GLORIOUS "TWELFTH"

No party is Complete without

GLOAG'S "GROUSE" BRAND WHISKY

One of the very best of SCOTCH WHISKIES.

retailing was changed forever. Both these trends accelerated after World War II, and by the 1960s and 70s were unstoppable.

As a relatively small, privately held Scottish business, Matthew Gloag & Son was far from immune from these market forces, but the company remained in family ownership until 1970. Three years previously, the sixth-generation Matthew Gloag had joined the firm but was shortly faced with the death of both of his parents. That tragic loss was compounded by the heavy taxation payable as death duties and it became inevitable that the firm had to be sold to pay these.

He turned to Highland Distillers, which for many years had supplied the principal high-quality single malts essential to the distinctive taste of The Famous Grouse. The fact that Highland was itself a Scottish company, almost exclusively concerned with whisky and fiercely determined to remain independent, made it the natural partner and, in 1970, ownership passed to it.

WORLDWIDE SUCCESS

At that time, total sales of The Famous Grouse were around 100,000 cases annually, but the new owners recognized the brand's great potential. In 1972, marketing support was increased and sales began to grow rapidly – to the landmark of one million cases in 1979; becoming Scotland's favourite whisky (a position it holds still) the following year, and by 1989 shipping more than two million cases annually. Such an achievement would never have been possible without the greater resources of Highland Distillers.

By 1999 sales had risen to more than 2.5 million cases – and Highland Distillers was itself absorbed by The Edrington Group. This meant that Matthew Gloag & Son was once again in private ownership. Ultimately the business belongs to a charity, The Robertson Trust, which itself had been established in 1961 to provide long-lasting protection for the Robertson family-owned distilling business, and especially assurance that the company would remain based in Scotland. As a result, many millions of pounds are distributed annually to benefit a wide range of good causes, principally in Scotland.

In a world of globalization, consolidation and international trade it is all too easy to lose sight of a company's origins and history. But The Famous Grouse, for all its global success, has not lost touch with its heritage, and a justified, and justifiable, sense of authenticity remains a major part of its appeal. Not for nothing has it remained Scotland's favourite whisky for more than 30 years!

HOW WHISKY
IS MADE

While Friar John Cor might be bemused at one of Scotland's present-day distilleries, an 18th-century Highland or Lowland distiller certainly would not. There is more technology to be found in today's distilleries but it is there to serve traditional principles and the fundamental science has not been altered – as indeed it cannot be.

Whisky is still made with simple ingredients: water, which Scotland has in abundance; yeast, which every cook will know and employ in breadmaking; and cereals: malted barley for single malt, a wider range for use in grain whisky.

The cereals used in whisky production contain fermentable sugars. These are released either by malting (for the distilling of single malt whisky) or by cooking (for grain whisky production), after which the grain is mixed with hot water to obtain a sweet liquid known as 'wort'. The residual 'spent grains' remaining from this process are then dried and sold as a nutritious cattle food: what the distiller is interested in is the wort, which is then transferred to large fermentation vessels where yeast is added.

Yeast is a living organism that loves to feed on sugar. Added to the liquid (by now it's referred to as 'wash') the yeast multiplies rapidly, giving off CO_2 gas and turning the liquid into a kind of beer. This generally takes between 48 and 96 hours, after which the wash is pumped to the still house. It is now typically around eight per cent abv (alcohol by volume) in strength – and this is where the magic really starts.

In a single malt distillery there are two types of stills: a larger wash still and a smaller spirit still. Both rely on the same fundamental principle: that alcohol boils

at a lower temperature than water. Accordingly, if a quantity of liquid of low alcoholic strength (our eight per cent abv wash) is gently heated to around 80°C the vapour (steam) that comes off the liquid is mainly alcohol. If this is collected and re-distilled the strength can be increased to around 70 per cent abv.

In the pot stills found in a single malt distillery, the vapour rises up the neck of the wash still and over to a condenser where, once again a liquid, it is collected and sent to the spirit still. Only the heart of the run, or the 'middle cut', is retained in a special spirit receiver. From here it is pumped to the filling store and collected in oak casks, which are sent to the warehouse.

There they will remain for a minimum of three years before the contents may be called 'Scotch whisky'. Some will be required for blending at this stage, but most whisky is allowed longer in the cask, quietly ageing and maturing all the while, adding depth and complexity to the flavour and colour to the whisky.

The same fundamental principle applies to the continuous distillation method, except that the still is very different in design and much stronger alcohol can be collected. Here again the new spirit is stored in oak barrels and must wait at least three years before it may be used for blending.

The distillation of single-malt whisky is still a hand-crafted batch process, guided as much by custom and practice as by science, and today still continues to work on the principles laid down by Aeneas Coffey more than 180 years ago.

What has changed is the scale of the industry and the consistency of its products. The early pioneers

served a local market; their efforts were modest in volume, and outside of its home, Scotch whisky was for much of its history known little and appreciated less. Men like Matthew Gloag and his successors changed that, building a worldwide success story – today exports of Scotch whisky are worth nearly £3.5 billion a year to the UK economy (that's around £109 a second) and Scotch whisky, especially premium blends such as The Famous Grouse, is finding new popularity in markets such as Brazil, Russia, India and China.

In part this is due to the greater consistency and reliability of the products produced today. With their increased understanding of the scientific processes involved in distilling and maturation, the industry's distillers and Master Blenders have been able steadily to increase the quality of whisky offered to the market. Today The Famous Grouse Master Blender is responsible for a complex process of quality control that stretches from malting to distillery, laboratory and sample room to warehouse to bottling hall to retail shelf as part of the staggering 8,000+ quality

checks that go to ensure the blend is consistent and of the highest quality. From cask to glass, every drop has been checked and checked again.

Along the way it's worth noting that a key part of the blending process at The Famous Grouse is known as 'marrying', a process that allows the individual malts and grains in the blend to gently harmonize by letting them rest together in cask for several months prior to bottling. The whisky is smoother, more mellow and better balanced. Unusually, the whiskies in The Famous Grouse blend can spend as long as six months in this stage. Not every distiller does this: it is time-consuming and expensive, but the result is well worth the time and trouble.

What is more there is no harsh 'chill filtering' prior to bottling, with the inevitable loss of some of the natural flavour particles that give the whisky its distinctive flavour and mouth feel. Instead, The Famous Grouse is only lightly filtered (at +4°C) – the flavours are preserved whilst an attractive bright colour is ensured.

THE FAMOUS GROUSE FAMILY

As we have seen, it helps that the Master Blender at The Famous Grouse has access to superb stocks of some of Scotland's finest single malt whiskies, which lend their distinctive flavours to the finished product. The existence of these whiskies, notably The Macallan, Highland Park, The Glenrothes and, of course, The Glenturret, has permitted the blending team to innovate and experiment. A remarkable range of whiskies has been the result.

THE FAMOUS GROUSE

Appearance
Full, golden, clear and bright

Aroma
Well balanced oak,
sherry with a citrus hint

Taste
Medium full flavour,
mature, Speyside fruitiness

Finish
Good length, clean and medium dry

The original is The Famous Grouse, today one of the best-selling Scotch whiskies in the world. Scotland's favourite whisky is a blend crafted from the finest malt whiskies, such as The Macallan and Highland Park, married with exceptional grain whiskies, for the smoothest possible taste. It is characterized by a full, golden, bright appearance and its balance of flavours, with a hint of citrus fruit, provides the distinctively long and clean finish.

This is an easy-to-drink whisky with superb balance. It pays tribute to the skill of the blenders, and the quality of the base whiskies shines through. Whether drunk neat, over ice or in a cocktail, The Famous Grouse will delight the connoisseur and is a great ambassador for Scotland.

It has justifiably won many awards. Just a few of the most recent include:

* Scotch Whisky Masters 2009 – Gold Award

* Scotch Whisky Masters 2008 – Silver Award

* San Francisco World Spirits Competition
  2008 – Silver Medal

* San Francisco World Spirits Competition
  2006 – Silver Medal

* International Wine and Spirits Competition
  2007 – Silver Medal

THE BLACK GROUSE

Appearance
Dark, russet golden, clear and bright

Aroma
Smoky, soft, musky, rich and full

Taste
Full flavour, spice and dried fruits, smoke through the oak, with all The Famous Grouse smoothness

Finish
Long, smoky and aromatic

In line with the fashion of more heavily peated whiskies, The Black Grouse was introduced to cater for those drinkers looking for a smokier, but smooth, taste.

The Black Grouse takes the base of the flagship blend but adds specially selected peated malts to create a rich, dark, russet whisky with a rich, soft, smoky nose. On the palate, the peaty character comes through in spice and dried fruit flavours, and late smoky oak that leaves a long aromatic finish.

Like its big brother, this too has been widely acclaimed in international competition.

* Scotch Whisky Masters 2009 – Gold Medal

* Scotch Whisky Masters 2009 – Best Premium Blend – Silver Medal

* International Spirits Challenge 2008 – Gold Medal

* International Spirits Challenge 2007 – Silver Medal

* International Spirits Challenge 2007 – Silver Medal

THE SNOW GROUSE

Appearance
Straw, clear and bright

Aroma
Soft creamy vanilla, cloudy honey, nutmeg and lightly oaky

Taste
Smooth and sweet vanilla fudge

Finish
Sweet and lingering

The blending team did not leave their restless exploration there. The Snow Grouse is a most unusual whisky, as it uses only single grain whiskies from the continuous still in what is known as 'blended grain'. This might just be Scotland's best-kept whisky secret.

The whiskies are matured in oak casks and then gently chill filtered in a unique filtration process, designed so that The Snow Grouse is perfectly at home in severely cold conditions. In fact, in breach of all whisky tradition, it's recommended that you serve this straight from the freezer. At first it seems quite viscous, but look out for an explosion of taste as it warms in your mouth.

It too has enjoyed its share of recent awards, including:

* Drinks International – Best Blended Whisky 2008

* Duty Free News International – Highly Commended – Best New Liquor and Wines Product 2008

THE NAKED GROUSE

Appearance
Polished, rich dark mahogany, hinting at the extra sherry cask maturation

Aroma
Dried fruits, vanilla sweetness and spice hints

Taste
Chocolate; buttery, vanilla cream; mixed fruits; sherry and vanilla; delicate floral notes

Finish
Medium length, oak, chocolate, a wisp of peat and spice lingers

The Naked Grouse is the most recent addition to the family. As the name suggests, it comes in minimalist packaging – just the rather handsome bottle, with a simple neck label to hint at the pleasure within. The blend is distinguished by the extra smoothness delivered by a high percentage of sherry casks used and the influence of The Macallan and Highland Park single malts.

Already an award winner …

'This [The Naked Grouse] was an instant favourite. Its sweet, almost toffee like nose demanded to be tasted – and there was no disappointment. It has a great after taste of all things that you'd expect from a Scotch plus a hint of smoke – dangerously moorish [*sic*].'
Patience Gould, Editor of Spirits Business *and Chair of the Scotch Whisky Masters*

* Winner of best new expression 2010/11 – Scottish Field Whisky Challenge

RECIPES

GLENTURRET DISTILLERY – HOME OF THE FAMOUS GROUSE

The Glenturret distillery is to be found just outside
Crieff, a charming small market town in the heart
of the Perthshire countryside.

The distillery was established in 1775, making it the
oldest in Scotland. Like so many others, it went through periods
of both prosperity and adversity as whisky's fortunes fluctuated
in line with fashion and the economy. After a long silent period in
the twentieth century it was re-opened in 1959 by James Fairlie
and has been distilling continuously ever since.

Today, it is owned by The Edrington Group, one of Scotland's
most respected distilling companies. As proprietors of The
Famous Grouse they have made Glenturret the 'home of
The Famous Grouse' and, in May 2002, opened The Famous
Grouse Experience Centre.

Today, you are welcome to visit Glenturret to see
how whisky is made and learn some of the secrets
of Scotland's most popular dram. Enthusiastic visitors
can even join the centre's Cook School or Whisky School for
some expert tuition.

pepper

salt

POULTRY, GAME & MEAT

garlic

EXTRA
Virgin
olive oil

THE
FAMOUS
GROUSE

THE FAMOUS GROUSE CONSOMMÉ

The Famous Grouse consommé garnished with garden
vegetables and pheasant and mushroom quenelles.

Serves 6–8

For the consommé
500 g minced mixed game
2 carrots, peeled and roughly chopped
2 celery sticks, roughly chopped
2 onions, roughly chopped
1 bouquet garni
2 fresh rosemary sprigs
2 fresh thyme sprigs
550 ml beef stock
50 ml (2 drams) The Famous Grouse
Salt and freshly ground black pepper

For the quenelles
2 boneless skinless pheasant breasts
50 g wild mushrooms
25 g fresh tarragon
1 medium egg
200 ml cream
550 ml good-quality chicken stock
Salt and freshly ground black pepper

For the vegetable garnish
2 celery sticks, very finely diced
2 carrots, very finely diced
1 leek, very finely diced
10 rosemary sprigs

mushrooms

Place all the ingredients for the consommé except the beef stock and whisky in a tall stock pot and fill with 2 litres of water. Heat to boiling point, then reduce the temperature until the liquid reaches 80°C (a sugar thermometer is good to check this with). Keep the consommé at this temperature for about 3 hours. Do not stir at any time during this period.

To make the quenelles, place the pheasant breasts, mushrooms and tarragon into a food processor and blitz until well mixed. Add the egg and cream, season with salt and pepper and blitz until the mixture is smooth with no lumps.

Place the chicken stock into a pan, bring to a boil then reduce until simmering. Form the pheasant mixture into quenelle-shaped dumplings using 2 teaspoons and drop a few at a time into the stock. Leave to simmer for 10 minutes until cooked. Keep the dumplings warm while cooking the next batch. This mixture should make about 20–25 dumplings.

While the quenelles are cooking, strain the consommé through a muslin cloth into a clean pan. Pour in the beef stock to colour, check the seasoning, add the whisky, diced vegetables and rosemary sprig and simmer for a further 8 minutes.

To serve, ladle the consommé into bowls, remove the dumplings from the chicken stock and add to the consommé to garnish.

ST ANDREW'S CHICKEN

Chicken breast stuffed with haggis, wrapped in smoked bacon and
served with whisky fondant potato, glazed baby vegetables
and The Famous Grouse and thyme jus.

Serves 4

For the glazed baby vegetables
12 baby carrots
4 baby turnips, quartered
8 baby courgettes
3 tsp honey
20 g butter

For the fondant potatoes
4 medium baking potatoes, peeled
80 g butter
25 ml (1 dram) The Famous Grouse
200 ml good-quality chicken stock
1 fresh rosemary sprig, chopped
Salt and freshly ground black pepper

For the chicken
4 boneless skinless chicken breasts
80 g haggis
8 slices smoked streaky bacon
1 litre good-quality chicken stock
20 g butter
1 garlic clove, crushed
Salt and freshly ground black pepper

For The Famous Grouse
& thyme jus
20 g butter
1 carrot, chopped
1 onion, chopped
½ leek, chopped
3 celery sticks, chopped
50 ml (2 drams) The Famous Grouse
400 ml strong good-quality beef stock
1 tsp tomato purée
2 fresh thyme sprigs, chopped
1 bay leaf
1 clove
20 g butter

Preheat the oven to 190°C (gas mark 5). First blanch the carrots and turnips. Bring a pan of salted water to the boil. Drop in the turnips and continue to boil. After 1 minute, drop in the carrots. Cook for a further minute, then drain the vegetables and run under cold water to cool. Set aside.

To make the fondant potatoes, using a cutter, square off the ends of the potatoes to create a flat surface. Using a scone cutter, cut each potato into a cylinder shape approximately 4 cm high and 6 cm in diameter. Trim any excess with a small knife if necessary. Melt half the butter in an ovenproof pan, and brown the potatoes top and bottom, until they have a bit of colour. Deglaze the pan with whisky, then pour the stock over the potatoes. Scatter with rosemary and season. Put a small piece of butter on top of each potato then cover with foil and cook in the oven for about 45 minutes until tender.

Meanwhile, slice open each chicken breast horizontally, place 20 g of haggis in the centre and season. Close the chicken breast over the filling and wrap with 2 slices of streaky bacon. Wrap each breast tightly in cling film, twisting the ends firmly to seal. Place the chicken stock into a pan large enough to fit the 4 chicken breasts, and bring the stock to a boil. Drop in the wrapped chicken breasts and simmer for 16–18 minutes until cooked. Remove from the pan and remove the cling film. Heat the butter and crushed garlic in a large frying pan and gently fry the chicken until golden brown. Keep warm until ready to serve.

To make the jus, heat the butter in another pan and sauté the chopped carrot, onion, leek and celery until softened. Deglaze the pan with whisky, then add the beef stock, tomato purée, thyme, bay leaf and clove. Bring to a boil then reduce until thickened slightly – this will take about 5 minutes – then strain. Whisk in the butter to emulsify the sauce and keep warm until ready to serve.

For the glazed vegetables, sauté the baby courgettes in the butter until al dente, then add the blanched carrots and turnips and warm for 2–3 minutes. Glaze with honey and butter and season to taste.

To serve, cut 3 slices into each chicken breast, lay the fondant potato beside it on a plate and garnish with the glazed vegetable and whisky jus.

DUCK À LA GROUSE WITH BRAISED RED CABBAGE & FONDANT POTATOES

Serves 4

4 small duck breasts
300 g spinach leaves
2 garlic cloves, crushed
20 g butter

For the braised red cabbage
20 ml olive oil
400 g red cabbage, finely chopped
2 small onions, finely chopped
1 fresh thyme sprig, chopped
1 garlic clove, crushed
20 g brown sugar
75 ml red wine

For the fondant potato
4 large baking potatoes, peeled
75 g butter
25 ml (1 dram) The Famous Grouse
200 ml good-quality chicken stock
Sprig of rosemary
Salt and freshly ground black pepper

For the orange sauce
90 g caster sugar
90 ml red wine vinegar
700 ml blood orange juice or
orange juice
75 ml (3 drams) The Famous Grouse
375 ml chicken stock
Zest of 1 large orange
75 g butter, diced
Salt and freshly ground black pepper

Preheat the oven to 180°C (gas mark 4). Start by making the braised red cabbage. Heat the olive oil in a heavy-based pan, then, over a medium heat, add the cabbage, onion and thyme and sweat for a few minutes. Add the garlic, cook for a further 1 minute, then add the brown sugar and red wine. Cover the pan with a tightly fitting lid and braise over a very low heat for about an hour, stirring every 10 minutes or so.

To make the fondant potatoes, square off each potato to create a 6-cm-square piece. Melt half the butter in an ovenproof pan and brown the potatoes on all sides. Deglaze the pan with the whisky, then pour the stock over the potatoes. Scatter over rosemary and seasoning. Place a knob of the remaining butter on top of each potato, then cover with foil and cook in the oven for about 45 minutes, or until tender.

To make the orange sauce, place the sugar in a cold pan and heat gently, being careful not to let it burn. When it starts to dissolve, add the vinegar and simmer until the sugar has completely dissolved. Stir in the orange juice and whisky and simmer until the sauce has reduced by half. Add the chicken stock and reduce by half again. Add the orange zest and whisk in the butter to thicken the sauce slightly. Season to taste.

Place the duck skin side down in a smoking hot frying pan and cook until the fat has been released and the skin is crispy and dark golden brown. This will take 2 or 3 minutes. Turn the duck over and cook over a medium heat for a further 6–8 minutes. Remove from the heat and allow to rest in a warm place for 5 minutes.

Wilt the spinach in the butter with the garlic, and heat up the sauce, just before serving.

To serve, slice each duck breast into 3 equal slices, place the fondant potato off centre on each plate, place a generous mound of braised cabbage next to it, place the spinach on the other side of the plate and set the sliced duck on top of the spinach. Finally, drizzle with the orange sauce.

PAN-FRIED PHEASANT BREAST WITH WILD MUSHROOM SALAD

Serves 4

4 pheasant breasts
Olive oil
Salt and freshly ground black pepper

**For The Famous Grouse &
fig chutney**
400 ml red wine
200 ml balsamic vinegar
50 ml (2 drams) The Famous Grouse
4 tbsp sugar
2 shallots diced
12 large figs, each cut into 8
25 g coriander, roughly chopped

For the wild mushroom salad
300 g assorted wild mushrooms
30 ml olive olive oil
6 tbsp lime juice
4 tbsp soy sauce
½ tsp chilli powder
4 shallots, sliced
4 spring onions, finely sliced
1 tbsp fresh mint, roughly chopped
1 tbsp fresh coriander,
roughly chopped

To make the fig chutney, put the red wine, balsamic vinegar, whisky, sugar and the diced shallots in a pan, bring to a boil and simmer until reduced by half. Add the figs and cook until softened and easy to crush, about 2–3 minutes. Remove the pan from the heat, crush the figs with a fork and stir in the chopped coriander.

To make the wild mushroom salad, wipe clean the mushrooms and cut any large ones into thick slices. Heat the olive oil in a medium pan, add the mushrooms and sauté for a few minutes, until lightly coloured. Remove the pan from the heat and season the mushrooms with the lime juice, soy sauce and chilli powder. Add the shallots, spring onions and herbs, and keep warm.

Season the pheasant and pan-fry in a little olive oil over a medium heat for 2 minutes on each side, until pink in the centre. Allow to rest for 3 minutes.

To serve, divide the mushroom salad between 4 plates, slice the pheasant breasts in half diagonally and place on top of the mushrooms, and top with fig chutney.

mushrooms

salt

THE BLACK GROUSE VENISON

Fillet of venison on a pearl barley risotto garnished
with rosemary and The Black Grouse jus.

Serves 4

4 x 200 g strips of loin of venison
100g mixed fresh herbs, chopped
(e.g. parsley, tarragon, chives)
Freshly ground black pepper
Truffle oil, to drizzle (optional)

For the barley risotto
1 tbsp olive oil
½ onion, finely chopped
1 garlic clove, crushed
1 leek, finely chopped
200 g barley, rinsed
Grated zest of 1 orange
4 fresh rosemary sprigs, chopped
600 ml good-quality lamb stock
150 ml red wine
2 eating apples, peeled,
cored and diced
Salt and freshly ground black pepper

For The Black Grouse jus
40 g butter, cubed
1 carrot, diced
1 onion, diced
½ leek, diced
3 celery sticks, diced
50 ml (2 drams) The Black Grouse
400 ml good-quality beef stock
1 tsp tomato purée
2 fresh thyme sprigs
1 bay leaf
2 cloves

garlic

Season the venison with salt and pepper and set aside. Preheat the oven to 220°C (gas mark 7).

To make the risotto, heat the oil in a heavy-based pan. Add the onion, garlic and leek and cook gently until softened. Add the pearl barley and cook until it starts to turn pale brown. Stir in the orange zest and rosemary, then pour in the stock and wine and bring to a boil. Reduce to a gentle simmer, cover and cook for 40–50 minutes, or until the barley has soaked up liquid and has bite to it. If the liquid is aborbed before the barley is cooked, just add a little water occasionally to finish cooking. Stir in the apple and cover with a lid.

Meanwhile, make the jus: heat half the butter in a pan and sauté the diced carrot, onion, leek and celery until softened. Deglaze the pan with the whisky then add the beef stock, tomato purée, thyme, bay leaf and cloves. Bring to a boil, simmer until reduced by about a third, achieving a sauce-like consistency, then strain. Whisk in the remaining butter to emulsify the sauce, and keep warm.

Heat a little olive oil in an ovenproof pan. Seal the venison on all sides and place the pan in the oven for about 5 minutes to finish cooking (until the venison is medium rare). Once cooked, remove from the oven and leave to rest for 3 minutes, then roll each strip-loin steak in herbs and cracked black pepper.

To serve, place a large cutter in the centre of a plate and fill with risotto, then carefully remove the cutter. Slice each venison loin into 3 equal slices and tower on top of the risotto. Garnish with The Black Grouse jus. Drizzle with a few drops of truffle oil to enhance the flavour if desired.

MEET THE GROUSE

The red grouse (Scotland's national game bird) first appeared on a whisky label in 1896 and rapidly took off! In 1905, fittingly on 12 August in fact, 'The Famous' was added to the name and history was made. But what of the bird itself?

The red grouse (or *Lagopus lagopus scoticus* to give it its Sunday name) is found all across the UK but is principally associated with Scotland, where it inhabits mainly upland heather moors. The bird is completely wild, and attempts to rear it in captivity have failed.

Throughout the year its plumage is handsome reddish brown, set off by the black tail and striking white legs with white stripes on the underwing and red combs over the eye. The modest females are less reddish than the cock bird and have smaller combs.

With its distinctive cry of 'Goback, goback, goback' and rapidly whirring flight when disturbed, the red grouse is highly regarded as a game bird and as a symbol of Scotland's wilder places.

THE SECRET'S IN THE WOOD

All whisky spends at least three years stored in
Scotland in an oak cask. It's the law, and the spirit
can't be called 'Scotch' until the three years are up.

But there are casks and there are casks: not all are
equal. A lot of the flavour in whisky comes from the
wood, and it stands to reason, the better the wood,
the better the whisky.

Fortunately for drinkers of The Famous Grouse, the single malt
whiskies that go into the blend spend their years of maturation
in some of the best wood that can be found. The blenders are
notorious in the industry for their demanding approach (rivals
would call it 'pernickety'), insisting on the finest sherry-and
bourbon-seasoned barrels that money can buy.

Nothing is left to chance, and the maturing whisky is checked
regularly. The result? Unparalleled smoothness and depth of
flavour, with not a harsh note in a drop.

No need to touch wood here. That's already been done!

THE FAMOUS GROUSE RACK OF LAMB

Rack of lamb served with apple and grape chutney,
dauphinoise potatoes and puy lentil and rosemary jus.

Serves 6

30 ml olive oil
6 x 3-bone racks of lamb
Rock salt and freshly ground
black pepper

For the dauphinoise potatoes
20 g butter
900 g waxy potatoes
150 ml whole milk
150 ml double cream
1 garlic clove, crushed
2 fresh thyme sprigs
Pinch of freshly ground nutmeg

For the apple and grape chutney
6 apples, peeled and diced
200 g red grapes, halved
3 garlic cloves, crushed
6 tbsp balsamic vinegar
3 tbsp sherry
3 tbsp honey
175 ml red wine
175 ml good-quality chicken stock

For the puy lentil jus
1 small onion, chopped
1 carrot, peeled and diced
1 celery stick, diced
50 ml (2 drams) The Famous Grouse
400 ml good-quality lamb stock
1 bouquet garni
3 tbsp puy lentils, cooked
3 fresh rosemary sprigs
30 g butter

Preheat the oven to 180°C (gas mark 4). Start by making the dauphinoise potatoes. Line an 8 cm square baking tin with greaseproof paper and butter the paper. Peel the potatoes and cut them into slices about 3 mm thick, then pat dry with kitchen paper.

Pour the milk and cream into a pan and add the garlic and thyme. Bring to a boil, then remove from the heat, leave to cool a little and strain into a jug. Sprinkle with nutmeg and keep warm.

Layer half the potatoes in the tin, overlapping the slices and sprinkling each layer with salt and pepper. Pour over half the liquid and finish layering, then add the remaining liquid. Bake in the oven for 1–1¼ hours, or until the potatoes are tender and the top is golden.

To make the chutney, put all the ingredients into a pan and simmer for about 5 minutes, or until soft and tender, stirring occasionally. Keep warm.

When the potatoes are cooked, remove them from the oven and keep warm. Increase the oven temperature to 190°C (gas mark 5). Heat the olive oil in a large frying pan and seal 3 racks of lamb at a time, ensuring they are lightly browned on all sides. Remove the racks from the pan and place, well separated, in an ovenproof dish and set aside. Keep the pan containing the lamb juices and residue to make the jus.

To make the puy lentil jus, put the onion, carrot and celery into the reserved pan and sweat for 5 minutes. Deglaze the pan with the whisky, then add the lamb stock and bouquet garni and reduce until the sauce coats the back of a spoon. Strain the sauce then add the puy lentils, rosemary and butter and season to taste.

Season the lamb, place on a baking sheet in the oven and cook for about 10–12 minutes (it should be pink in the middle). Remove from the oven and leave to rest for 5 minutes.

To serve, slice the dauphinoise potatoes into 6 equal portions and place on warm plates. Slice the lamb racks between the bones and place beside the potatoes. Spoon a generous portion of chutney onto each plate and garnish with the puy lentil jus.

THE FAMOUS GROUSE STOVIES

Braised lamb shank topped with celeriac mash and served with crisp green salad and warmed oatcakes.

Serves 4

For the lamb shanks
30 ml olive oil
4 lamb shanks
2 carrots, chopped
2 celery sticks, chopped
2 onions, chopped
2 garlic cloves, chopped
½ bottle red wine
4 fresh rosemary sprigs
2 bay leaves
50 g parsley
Salt and freshly ground black pepper

For the lamb jus
400 ml good-quality strong lamb stock
2 tsp tomato purée
2 tsp sugar
50 g butter

For the celeriac mash
100 g butter
1 kg celeriac, peeled and grated
50 ml (2 drams) The Famous Grouse
200 ml double cream
2 tbsp coarse-grain mustard
Salt and freshly ground black pepper

To serve
8 triangle oatcakes, warmed and dusted with freshly grated nutmeg
Green salad leaves dressed with oil and vinegar

Heat the olive oil in a frying pan and brown the lamb shanks until coloured, then season. Remove from the pan and put into a deep casserole dish in which all 4 shanks can stand up.

Using the same pan, sweat the carrot, celery, onion and garlic for 5 minutes and place in the casserole dish with the lamb shanks. Deglaze the pan with the red wine and pour into the casserole. Add the herbs and fill with water to cover the meat of the shanks. Place on the hob, cover with a lid and bring to a boil, then gently simmer for 2–3 hours, or until the meat falls away from the bone.

When cooked, remove the lamb from the liquid, flake the meat from the bones and put it into an ovenproof dish. Skim the fat off the liquid remaining in the casserole, add the lamb stock and simmer until reduced by one third. Stir in the tomato purée and sugar and simmer until the liquid starts to thicken, then remove the casserole from the heat and add butter to finish. Pour over the lamb to cover the meat. Preheat the oven to 180°C (gas mark 4).

To make the celeriac mash, melt the butter in a pan, then add the celeriac. Cover the pan and sweat slowly for 8–10 minutes, or until softened, stirring frequently. When the celeriac is cooked, add the whisky and stir. Fold in the cream and continue to stir, cooking gently until the cream has been absorbed, then stir in the mustard and season to taste.

Spread the celeriac mash over the lamb in the casserole dish and bake in the oven for about 20 minutes, or until the mash is golden and the sauce is bubbling up around the edges of the dish.

Serve the stovies with warmed oatcakes, dusted with a little nutmeg, and a crisp green salad.

PORK LOIN AND STORNAWAY BLACK PUDDING

Pork loin stuffed with black pudding and set on Savoy cabbage, garnished with The Snow Grouse apple sauce. Ask your butcher to butterfly the pork loin for you.

Serves 4

1 kg pork loin, butterflied
200 g Stornaway black pudding
2 tbsp chopped fresh parsley
2 tbsp chopped fresh tarragon
Salt and freshly ground black pepper

For the Savoy cabbage
50 g butter
½ Savoy cabbage, finely shredded
2 eating apples, peeled, cored and diced
75 ml white wine
4 rashers streaky bacon, cooked and cut into thin strips
100 ml double cream
1 tbsp pine nuts, toasted
Salt and freshly ground black pepper

For The Snow Grouse apple sauce
1 kg cooking apples, peeled, cored and quartered
25 g dark brown sugar
25 g granulated sugar
2 strips of fresh lemon peel
Juice of 1 lemon
75 ml water
½ tsp salt
25 ml (1 dram) The Snow Grouse

Preheat the oven to 180°C (gas mark 4). Season inside the butterflied pork loin.

Remove the skin from the black pudding, break it into chunks and place it in a roasting tin in the oven for a couple of minutes to loosen its texture. Remove from the oven, place in a bowl, add the herbs and mix these well into the pudding. Reform into a sausage shape and place it in the centre of the pork. Roll the pork around the sausage and tie it up with string.

Place the pork in an ovenproof dish and cook in the oven for approximately 1–1¼ hours. (It should reach a core temperature of 70°C. Check the temperature with a meat probe if you have one; the meat juices should run clear.)

While the pork is cooking, prepare the cabbage and the apple sauce. To make the cabbage, melt the butter in a pan and gently cook the cabbage and apple for 5 minutes. Add the white wine, bacon and cream and slowly cook until the cream has reduced and the ingredients are binding together. Taste, season and keep warm. Fold through pine nuts just before serving.

To make the apple sauce, put all the ingredients except The Snow Grouse into a large pan. Cover and bring to a boil, then lower the heat and simmer for 10–15 minutes. Remove from the heat and remove and discard the strips of lemon peel. Put the sauce and The Snow Grouse into a food processor and purée until smooth. Taste and season.

Take the pork out of the oven and let it rest for 5 minutes before slicing. To serve, place some Savoy cabbage in the centre of each plate, lay slices of pork on top, then garnish with The Snow Grouse apple sauce.

HAGGIS WITH NEEPS & TATTIES

Haggis can now be found in many butchers and supermarkets around the world, but you can order one online and have it delivered if you wish. Buy the best quality you can find.

Serves 6

1.2 kg haggis
25 ml (1 dram) The Famous Grouse,
to serve

For the tatties (potatoes)
900 g potato, peeled and
roughly chopped
120 ml milk
90 g butter
Generous pinch of grated nutmeg
Sea salt

For the neeps (swede or turnip)
900 g turnip (or yellow swede),
peeled and roughly chopped
90 g butter
Sea salt and freshly ground
black pepper

Place the haggis into a large saucepan and cover it with cold water. Bring the water to a boil then reduce the heat to a gentle steady simmer and cover the pan. Leave the haggis to cook for 1½ hours (or 40 minutes per 500 g).

While the haggis is cooking, prepare the tatties and the neeps. Place the potatoes and turnip or swede in two separate saucepans and cover with cold water. Bring the water to a boil then reduce it to a strong simmer. Leave the potatoes to cook for 15–20 minutes and the turnip or swede to cook for 20–25 minutes, until they are tender. Drain the vegetables well and return to their pans.

Warm the butter and milk for the tatties in a small pan until the butter has melted. Meanwhile, mash the potatoes with a fork or potato masher. Pour over the butter and milk mixture and beat to a smooth mash. Stir in the nutmeg and season to taste.

Add the butter to the turnip or swede and mash with a fork or potato masher. Season the neeps with a little salt and pepper and beat until smooth.

To serve, remove the haggis from the pan and cut it open with scissors or a knife (it will be very hot). Serve the haggis heaped on warmed plates, drizzle a little of The Famous Grouse over each serving, and accompany with the mashed tatties and neeps and a generous dram!

THE FAMOUS GROUSE SUMMER STEAK

Fillet steak set on a watercress and rocket salad garnished with chargrilled courgettes and blue cheese pesto dressing.

Serves 2

2 medium courgettes
2 x 170 g fillet steaks
25 g (1 dram) The Famous Grouse
Rock salt and freshly ground
black pepper

For the salad
½ bunch asparagus
100 g rocket
100 g watercress
½ red onion, finely sliced
1 small avocado, sliced
2 tomatoes, diced
2 tsp chopped chives
2 tsp grated Parmesan
Salt and freshly ground black pepper
15 ml olive oil, to serve

For the blue cheese pesto dressing
30 ml olive oil
50 g Parmesan, finely grated
25 g blue cheese
25 g basil
1 tbsp pine nuts, toasted
Pinch of salt and freshly ground
black pepper

Preheat the oven to 200°C (gas mark 6). To make the salad, blanch the asparagus in boiling water for 2 minutes, drain and run cold water over the asparagus to cool. In a large bowl, mix together all the salad ingredients, then drizzle with the olive oil.

To make the blue cheese pesto dressing, place all the ingredients into a food processor or blender and blend until smooth. Add more olive oil if the consistency is too thick.

Slice each courgette in half lengthways and rub the cut side with a few drops of olive oil. Heat a chargrilling pan to smoking hot, then place the courgette cut side down in the pan for 3 minutes. Turn the courgettes over and cook for a further 2 minutes. If you don't have a chargrill pan, grill under a very hot grill for the same cooking times.

Season the steaks with salt and pepper. Heat an ovenproof frying pan until smoking and seal the steaks in the pan for 1 minute on each side. Remove the pan from the heat, add The Famous Grouse and swirl around. Pop the frying pan in the oven for 5 minutes for a medium-rare steak. Remove from the oven, cover with a plate and rest the steaks for 3 minutes.

To serve, place the courgette halves off centre on each plate and top with salad. Place the steak alongside the salad and garnish with the dressing.

ONLY THE BEST WILL DO
FOR THE FAMOUS GROUSE

One of the most important single malts that go to make up The Famous Grouse's distinctive taste is The Macallan, itself very highly regarded as a whisky in its own right. But did you know that The Macallan holds the record for the most expensive whisky in the world?

In November 2010, Sotheby's New York auctioned a stunning 1.5 litre Lalique crystal decanter containing the equivalent of two bottles of 64-year-old The Macallan for $460,000. This was the distillery's oldest and rarest whisky ever offered for sale and the competition from bidders at the auction was fierce.

The final price is the equivalent of more than £140,000 per single bottle, a record that seems unlikely to be broken for some time. What makes this remarkable figure all the more noteworthy is that every penny from the auction was donated to 'charity:water', an organization that provides access to clean, safe drinking water to people in developing nations.

We can all drink to that.

FISH &
SHELLFISH

ARBROATH SMOKIE TARTS

The Arbroath Smokie originated in the small fishing village of Auchmithie, made using whole haddock, tied in pairs and smoked over a hard wood fire, giving them their destinctive smoky flavour.

Serves 4

175 g shortcrust pastry
Flour, for dusting
1 Arbroath smokie (approx. 200 g)
2 medium eggs
200 ml crème fraîche
1 tbsp horseradish sauce
3 tsp oatmeal
Freshly ground black pepper
Steamed asparagus and cherry tomato salad,
to serve (optional)

Preheat the oven to 220°C (gas mark 7). Roll out the pastry on a lightly floured surface and line 4 10 cm loose-bottomed tart tins. To blind bake, line the tart cases with baking paper and fill with rice, dried beans or metal or ceramic baking weights. Place on a baking sheet and cook in the preheated oven for 8 minutes. Remove the pastry case from the oven and remove the paper and rice, dried beans or baking weights. Reduce the oven temperature to 180°C (gas mark 4) and cook for a further 5–10 minutes, or until light golden.

Meanwhile, remove the skin and bones from the Arbroath smokie and flake the flesh roughly. Divide the flaked fish between the cooled tart cases. Whisk together the eggs, crème fraîche, horseradish sauce and freshly ground black pepper. Pour over the fish and scatter the oatmeal over the top.

Reduce the oven temperature to 170°C (gas mark 3) and bake the tarts for 15 minutes, or until set and lightly brown on top. Serve warm, with steamed asparagus and cherry tomato salad.

SMOKED SALMON CRÊPES

Serves 4

For the crêpes
350 ml whole milk
50 g butter, melted
2 large eggs
110 g plain flour
Pinch of salt

For the filling
225 g cream cheese, softened
2 tbsp butter, softened
2 tbsp lemon zest
1 medium shallot, finely chopped

50 g capers, rinsed and chopped
20 g chopped dill
100 g baby spinach
2 tsp extra-virgin olive oil
2 tsp balsamic vinegar
12 slices smoked salmon
½ cucumber, thinly sliced
Salt and freshly ground black pepper

To serve
Wedges of lemon
Crispy salad leaves

In a bowl, whisk the milk with 75 ml water, the melted butter and the eggs. Mix the flour and salt in another bowl. Whisk the milk mixture into the flour and beat well with a balloon whisk, strain the batter through a sieve if there are any lumps, and refrigerate for 1 hour.

Heat a large frying pan over a medium heat. Melt a teaspoon of butter in the pan and swirl to coat the bottom. Pour 80 ml of the crêpe batter into the pan and swirl the pan to coat evenly with batter. Cook the crêpe until lightly golden on the bottom, about 2 minutes. Flip the crêpe and cook for a further minute until golden on the other side. Transfer the crêpe to a plate, cover with a clean tea towel to prevent drying out and repeat with the remaining batter.

For the filling, in a bowl, blend the cream cheese with the butter, lemon zest, shallot, capers, dill and seasoning. In a medium bowl, toss the spinach with the olive oil and balsamic vinegar. Fold each crêpe in half. Spread the cream cheese mixture on each crêpe. Lay the salmon over the cream cheese, top with the spinach salad and cucumber and season. Fold one side of the crêpe over the filling, roll to close and serve with a lemon wedge and crisp salad leaves.

THE FAMOUS GROUSE
HOT SMOKED SALMON

Hot smoked salmon set on a noodle and watercress salad with chargrilled asparagus and roasted lemon dressing. You will also need several large handfuls of uncoated sawdust (the type you get to put in a hamster cage) for smoking the salmon.

Serves 4

For the salmon
100 ml (4 drams) The Famous Grouse
4 tbsp honey
4 x 150 g salmon fillets
Rock salt and freshly ground
black pepper

For the roasted lemon dressing
4 lemons, halved
60 ml olive oil
1 tbsp honey
4 tbsp pine nuts, toasted
Salt and freshly ground
black pepper

**For the saffron noodle
& watercress salad**
280 g fine egg noodles
1 tbsp vegetable stock powder
Pinch of saffron

100 g watercress
1 small red onion, finely sliced
1 celery stick, finely sliced
3 tbsp chopped fresh coriander
12 cherry tomatoes, halved
Olive oil, to drizzle
4 tsp grated Parmesan
Salt and freshly ground
black pepper

To serve
1 bunch of asparagus,
chargrilled

Preheat the oven to 200°C (gas mark 6). In a small bowl, mix together The Famous Grouse and the honey. Place the salmon in a dish, pour over the whisky and honey mixture and marinate for up to 30 minutes for the flavours to infuse.

Next roast the lemons for the dressing. Cut the lemons in half, pick out and discard the seeds, and lightly coat with 1 tablespoon of the olive oil. Place them cut side down in a baking dish and roast, uncovered for 25 minutes.

While the lemons are still hot, squeeze the juice out into a bowl, add the honey and the remaining olive oil and whisk until the mixture forms a light dressing. Stir in the toasted pine nuts and season to taste.

To smoke the salmon, line the inside of a roasting tin with foil. Spread several large handfuls of uncoated sawdust evenly over the foil. Season the salmon fillets and place them skin side down on a cooling rack and place in the roasting tin. Make a tightly sealed lid with a double layer of foil to ensure that the smoke doesn't escape. Place the roasting tin on the hob over a medium heat for 8–10 minutes. After a couple of minutes it will start to smoke – don't be alarmed, just open the kitchen windows! Turn off the heat after 8–10 minutes. The salmon will keep warm until you're ready to serve it.

While the salmon is smoking, make the salad. Cook the noodles according to the packet instructions, adding the vegetable stock powder and pinch of saffron to the water. In a bowl, mix together the cooked warm noodles, watercress, red onion, celery, coriander, tomatoes and salt and pepper, then drizzle over olive oil and sprinkle with Parmesan.

Blanch the asparagus stems in boiling salted water for 1 minute. Drain and cool under cold running water. Heat a chargrill pan, toss the stems in a little olive oil and chargrill for 3–4 minutes, turning once. Alternatively toss the stems in a large frying pan to brown, for the same cooking time.

To serve, place the saffron noodle and watercress salad on the warmed plates, garnish with asparagus, top with the salmon and drizzle over the dressing.

MACKEREL WITH THE SNOW GROUSE PICKLED RHUBARB

Serves 2

4 mackerel fillets

Olive oil, for brushing

For the pickled rhubarb

200 g pink rhubarb, cut into
thin long slices

75 g caster sugar

30 ml white wine vinegar

50 ml (2 drams) The Snow Grouse

For the pea shoot salad

Handful of pea shoot leaves

¼ cucumber, finely diced

75 g fresh peas

1 tbsp olive oil

1 tsp balsamic vinegar

Salt and freshly ground black pepper

Preheat the oven to 200°C (gas mark 6). To make the pickled rhubarb, scatter the rhubarb slices on a baking sheet in a single layer. Sprinkle over the sugar and drizzle over the white wine vinegar and The Snow Grouse, then cover with foil. Bake in the oven for about 8 minutes, or until the rhubarb is just starting to soften but still keeping its shape. Remove to a shallow dish and leave the rhubarb to cool in its marinade.

To make the pea shoot salad, in a bowl, toss together the pea shoots, cucumber and fresh peas. Drizzle with olive oil and balsamic vinegar and season to taste.

Brush the mackerel fillets with a little olive oil. Place on a griddle pan, or in a large non-stick frying pan, over a medium heat, skin side down, for 2 minutes, then turn over and cook for another 2 minutes or until just cooked.

To serve, lay 2 mackerel fillets in the centre of each plate, place rhubarb slices around the plate and pour the pickling juices over the mackerel. Pile the salad on top of the fish.

TROUT WITH AN ORANGE AND FENNEL CRUST

Serves 4

3 tbsp fine dry breadcrumbs
½ tsp fennel seeds, coarsely chopped
½ tsp finely grated fresh orange zest
2 tbsp olive oil
4 rainbow trout fillets
4 tsp Dijon mustard
2 tsp The Famous Grouse
Salt and freshly ground black pepper

To serve (optional)
Broccoli and almond salad dressed
with crème fraîche
Steamed new potatoes

Preheat the oven to 220°C (gas mark 7). To make the crust mixture, in a small bowl, stir together the breadcrumbs, fennel seeds, orange zest, 1 tablespoon of the oil, ¼ teaspoon of salt and ¼ teaspoon of pepper until well combined.

Season the trout fillets. In a small bowl, stir together the mustard and The Famous Grouse. Use the remaining olive oil to lightly oil a baking sheet, then place the trout fillets skin side down on the baking sheet and spread evenly with the whisky and mustard mixture. Sprinkle a quarter of the breadcrumb mixture over each fillet. Roast the trout in the oven for 8-10 minutes until cooked through.

Serve with a broccoli and almond salad dressed with crème fraîche and steamed new potatoes, if desired.

Salt

THE SNOW GROUSE TUNA

Seared tuna steak served with wilted pak choi and The Snow Grouse,
kumquat and lime dressing.

Serves 4

300 g fresh tuna loin
50 g mixed fresh herbs, chopped
(e.g. parsley, tarragon, chives)
Salt and freshly ground black pepper

For the wilted pak choi
2 tsp olive oil
1 tsp grated fresh root ginger
1 large garlic clove, crushed
4 pak choi, halved lengthways

**For The Snow Grouse, kumquat
& lime dressing**
15 kumquats, halved and deseeded
3 limes, quartered
50 ml (2 drams) of The Snow Grouse
6 tbsp sugar
2 fresh rosemary sprigs
1 cinnamon stick
4 tbsp white wine vinegar

Season the tuna loin and set aside. Preheat the oven to 200°C (gas mark 6).

To make the dressing, heat a pan, toss in the kumquats and limes, pour in The Snow Grouse and flame. Once the flames have died down, add the sugar and 200 ml of water to the pan and bring to a boil. Add the rosemary and cinnamon stick and reduce to a simmer until the liquid reaches a light syrup consistency. Remove the rosemary and cinnamon, then place the kumquats and syrup in a food processor. Blitz until smooth then pass through a fine sieve. When cooled, stir in the white wine vinegar and season to taste.

For the pak choi, heat a large frying pan over a medium heat, add the olive oil, ginger and garlic and cook for 20 seconds. Add the pak choi and sauté until wilted, for about 3 minutes.

To cook the tuna, heat a frying pan until very hot, add the tuna loin and sear on all sides. Transfer to an ovenproof dish and cook in the oven for 4 minutes. Lay the chopped herbs out on a plate. Remove the tuna from the oven, roll it in the chopped herbs and slice into 4 equal portions.

To serve, place the pak choi in the centre of each plate, place a slice of tuna on top, and finish with the dressing.

SEA BASS WITH SAUCE VIERGE

Sea bass with a warm potato and kale salad and sauce vierge. This recipe can be doubled easily to serve 4 if necessary.

Serves 2

For the sauce vierge
50 ml olive oil
6 coriander seeds, crushed
2 tbsp lemon juice
1 tbsp finely chopped shallot
1 tbsp finely chopped fresh tarragon
1 tbsp finely chopped fresh chives
1 tbsp finely chopped fresh
coriander leaves
1 tbsp finely chopped tomato

For the sea bass
10 g butter
1 tbsp olive oil
2 x 160 g sea bass fillets
Juice of 1 lemon

For the warm potato & kale salad
150 g young kale leaves, washed
and shredded
200 g new potatoes, cooked and
quartered
1 tbsp olive oil
1 garlic clove, crushed
1 tbsp pine nuts, toasted

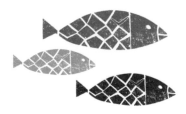

For the sauce, place all the ingredients in a small pan over a low heat until warmed slightly.

For the salad, bring a pan of water to a boil. Add the potatoes and the kale and cook for 2–3 minutes until the potatoes are hot and the kale tender. Drain and toss with the olive oil, garlic and pine nuts. Cover the pan with a lid to keep warm.

To cook the sea bass, heat the butter and oil in a large frying pan, add the sea bass fillets, skin side down, and pan fry for 2 minutes, until the skin is golden and crispy. Turn them over and fry for a further 1 minute, then remove the pan from the heat. Leave to rest for 1 minute then squeeze over the lemon juice.

To serve, place the potato and kale salad in the centre of the plate, lay the sea bass on top and pour over the sauce vierge.

SEAFOOD RAVIOLI WITH A CHIVE BUTTER SAUCE

Serves 4

For the pasta
300 g pasta flour, plus extra for dusting
3 eggs plus 3 egg yolks
Pinch of salt
1 tsp olive oil

For the seafood filling
250 g salmon fillet
250 g queen scallops, finely chopped
1 egg white
1 garlic clove, crushed
50 g white breadcrumbs
20 g fresh tarragon
Salt and freshly ground black pepper

For the chive butter sauce
220 g butter, clarified and still warm
2 egg yolks
20 ml sherry vinegar
Pinch of cayenne pepper
Pinch of salt
1 tsp lemon juice
20 g fresh chives, finely snipped

To make the pasta, place all the pasta ingredients into a food processor and pulse until they have formed a ball. Tip the dough onto a work surface and knead for 10 minutes, until smooth and elastic. Wrap in cling film and leave to rest for at least 20 minutes.

Meanwhile make the filling. Place all the ingredients in a food processor and blitz until bound together and well-combined.

To make the ravioli put the pasta dough on a lightly floured surface and roll as finely and evenly as possible (use a pasta machine if you have one). Roll into strips about 10 cm wide.

Place heaped teaspoonfuls of the filling on the pasta strips about 5 cm apart. Moisten the edges with water and cover with another strip of pasta. Press the pasta sheets together around the filling, sealing firmly, ensuring you don't trap any air. Cut into ravioli shapes using a pastry wheel or sharp knife. There should be at least 1 cm border around each piece of ravioli.

Next make the sauce; place the butter in a small saucepan and melt slowly. Meanwhile, blend the egg yolks, vinegar, cayenne and salt in a liquidizer or food processor. Then turn the heat up, and when the butter reaches a boil, pour it into a jug and start to pour this slowly into the liquidizer, in a thin trickle, with the motor running, until all the butter has been added and the sauce has thickened. With the motor still on, slowly add the lemon juice. Keep the sauce warm by placing it on a bowl over some hot water, covering with cling film.

Now cook the ravioli. Bring a large saucepan of salted water to the boil. Add the ravioli and cook for 4–6 minutes until al dente. Drain. Add the chives to the sauce, mix well and serve with the ravioli in shallow bowls.

Ravioli

STORING WHISKY

Whisky comes in a handy storage container, known as a bottle. As a distilled spirit it is effectively its own preservative and does not go 'off' once opened, unlike beer or wine, which are lower in strength.

Provided that it is kept upright and, for long-term storage out of direct sunlight, the flavour is unlikely to change noticeably. If unopened and still under the original seal, there is very little air in the bottle. The whisky cannot evaporate through the seal and it is stable for long-term storage.

Once the bottle has been opened, the more air in the bottle, the more the flavour can slowly change over time. Temperature variations and higher storage temperature will accelerate these effects, but the whisky should remain drinkable.

In fact, whisky has been recovered after being frozen in the Antarctic for around a hundred years and still found to be of perfectly acceptable quality.

That might be a little too much ice for most drinkers, however.

mushrooms

VEGETARIAN

garlic

cheese

SMOKED OYSTER MUSHROOM VELOUTÉ

Smoked oyster mushroom and The Black Grouse velouté,
garnished with truffle oil.

Serves 2

100 g oyster mushrooms
10 g butter
1 onion, finely diced
20 g flour
500 ml good-quality vegetable stock
25 ml (1 dram) The Black Grouse
100 ml cream
25 g parsley, finely chopped
Salt and freshly ground black pepper
Truffle oil, to serve

To smoke the mushrooms, line the inside of a roasting tin with foil. Spread several large handfuls of uncoated sawdust evenly over the foil. Season the mushrooms, put them on a cooling rack and place this in the roasting tin. Make a tightly sealed lid with a double layer of foil to ensure that the smoke doesn't escape. Place the roasting tin on the hob over a medium heat. After a couple of minutes it will start to smoke – don't be alarmed, just open the kitchen windows! Turn off the heat after 10 minutes.

Melt the butter in a large pan and sauté the onion until translucent. Add the flour and cook gently for a couple of minutes without colouring the paste. Add the stock and The Black Grouse, a little at a time, stirring until well blended. Simmer gently for about 5 minutes to ensure the flour is cooked and the mixture coats the back of a spoon, then pass it through a sieve and return it to the pan.

Add the smoked mushrooms and parsley and heat gently. Pour in the cream and simmer for 5 minutes. Before serving, blitz the velouté, using a handheld blender, until light and frothy. Pour into bowls and drizzle with truffle oil.

PORTOBELLO STUFFED MUSHROOMS

Serves 4

4 large portobello (flat) mushrooms
150 g couscous
150 ml vegetable stock, boiling
50 g sultanas
25 g pine nuts
1 garlic clove, crushed
Pinch of dried chilli flakes
70 g butter, melted
75 g smoked Cheddar, grated
Baby rocket leaves, to serve

Preheat the oven to 180°C (gas mark 4). Cut the stem from each mushroom and discard.

Put the couscous in a small bowl, pour over the boiling stock and cover the bowl with a plate. Leave for 5 minutes until the stock has been absorbed by the couscous.

Mix the sultanas, pine nuts, garlic, chilli flakes and melted butter into the couscous and fork until fluffy. Fill each mushroom with the mixture, packing it tightly. Sprinkle over the grated cheese.

Place the stuffed mushrooms onto a baking sheet and bake in the oven for 15–20 minutes, or until the cheese is bubbling. Serve hot, with some rocket leaves piled on top of each mushroom.

mushrooms

RED ONION AND GOATS'
CHEESE TARTLETS

Traditionally, Caesar dressing includes anchovy. If you're not making
this for vegetarians, finally chop an anchovy fillet, then rub it to a
paste on a board using the blade of a large knife and add this paste
to the bowl with the other dressing ingredients.

Serves 6 as a starter

500 g block shortcrust pastry
2 very large red onions
Dash of olive oil
1 glass red wine
1 tbsp balsamic vinegar
½ tbsp chopped thyme
6 slices of goats' cheese,
from a small log
18 Romaine lettuce leaves
Olive oil, to drizzle

For the Caesar dressing
1 fat garlic clove
1 anchovy fillet (optional, see above)
1 egg yolk
¼ tsp Dijon mustard
1 tbsp lemon juice
100 ml mild olive oil
2 tbsp grated Parmesan
½ tbsp double cream
Salt and freshly ground black pepper

Preheat the oven to 200°C (gas mark 6). Roll out the pastry, line 6 tart tins (about 10 cm diameter) and prick the bases. Line the pastry cases with baking paper and fill with baking beans, then bake for 10 minutes, or until the pastry starts to brown. Lift out the parchment and bake for a further 5 minutes, or until the pastry is crisp, dried and cooked.

Peel the red onions and slice them thickly into 1.5-cm-thick slices (you'll need 6 slices). Heat a little oil in a large frying pan and carefully fry the slices, without breaking them, on each side. Add the red wine, balsamic vinegar and thyme and bubble together, then transfer to the oven and cook for a further 10 minutes.

Lift a slice of onion into each tart and put a slice of goats' cheese on top. Return the tartlets to the oven and bake for 5–7 minutes, or until the goats' cheese has melted and turned golden brown.

Meanwhile, make the Caesar dressing. Crush the garlic clove under the blade of a large knife, rub it around the inside of a bowl, then discard. Add the egg yolk, mustard and lemon juice to the bowl and whisk until smooth. Slowly whisk in the olive oil, until creamy. Stir in the Parmesan, double cream and a little salt and pepper to taste.

To serve, combine the dressing with the Romaine lettuce leaves and divide the leaves between 6 plates. Set a tartlet on top of each, then drizzle with olive oil.

CRISPY PARSNIP FRITTERS

The batter for these fritters is made with a mixture of semolina flour and chickpea flour, both of which you should be able to find in a health food store or Asian supermarket. Don't try replacing the semolina flour with ordinary flour, as the latter is much coarser.

Serves 2

For the fritters
250 g parsnips, peeled
and finely grated
100 g chickpea flour
50 g semolina flour
1 tsp baking powder
1 tsp cumin seeds
1 tsp ground coriander
½ tsp turmeric
1 small red onion, finely chopped
2 red chillies, deseeded
and finely chopped
2 tsp grated fresh root ginger
Pinch of salt
60 ml vegetable oil, to fry
Salad leaves, to serve

For the dipping sauce
1 tbsp vegetable oil
1 tsp mild curry paste
1 green chilli, deseeded
and finely chopped
2 tsp grated fresh root ginger
Pinch of turmeric
200g thick Greek-style yoghurt
2 tbsp Scottish heather honey
1 tbsp grain mustard
2 tsp The Famous Grouse

First make the dipping sauce: heat the oil in a non-stick pan, add the curry paste and cook for 1 minute. Stir in the chilli, ginger and turmeric, cook over a low heat for 2–3 minutes, then leave to cool. Stir the cooled spice mix into the yoghurt along with the honey, mustard and whisky. Chill the sauce until you are ready to serve the fritters.

To make the fritters, in a large bowl, combine the grated parsnip, chickpea and semolina flours, baking powder, cumin seeds, coriander, turmeric, onion, chillies, ginger and salt. Pour in 200 ml cold water and mix until a thick batter is formed.

Heat a large non-stick frying pan and add 1 tablespoon of oil. When the oil is hot, drop a few tablespoons of the mixture into the pan to form a round pancake about 1–1.5 cm thick. Cook 2 or 3 pancakes at a time, for about 2–3 minutes, until they bubble on the surface and are golden brown on the bottom, then flip over and cook the other side until browned. Keep them warm while you make the rest. You should make 8 pancakes in total.

Place some salad leaves on 2 plates and arrange 4 fritters on top of each plate. Serve the pancakes with the honey, mustard and whisky dressing.

ginger

THROUGH A GLASS …

There is a lot to be said for using the right glass for any drink.
For whisky, the traditional tumbler is fine if you are using a mixer
or a lot of ice but hopeless for carefully considered tasting.

To really savour all the aromas (the whisky's 'nose') and fully
explore the taste, the best glass is probably a sherry copita or
brandy snifter. If you can get one, a specially designed whisky
tasting glass will really improve your experience. Fix the aroma
and taste with associations – the smell of new-mown grass, for
example; a vanilla-flavoured toffee or the rich taste of fruit cake.

Don't be afraid to add a little water. It opens up the spirit
and prevents your taste buds from becoming numbed by
alcohol. Give the flavours time to develop: the whisky has
been aging for years – give it as least as many seconds and
the rewards will be huge.

Finally, think about the lingering taste that remains. How
consistent is it? What new flavours emerge?

Relax, keep practising and you'll very soon discover whisky's
unique richness.

BEETROOT, FETA &
CARAMELIZED ONION FLAN

Serves 4

For the pastry
175 g wholemeal flour
100 g rolled porridge oats
100 g butter
100 g carrots, grated

For the filling
1 tbsp olive oil
3 large onions, peeled and
finely sliced

1 tbsp caster sugar
3 medium fresh beetroot,
peeled and grated
3 medium eggs
250 ml whole milk
Leaves from 2 fresh thyme sprigs
Salt and freshly ground black pepper
125g feta, crumbled

To serve
Baby leaf salad
Crusty baguette

Preheat the oven to 180°C (gas mark 4). Put the flour, oats and butter in a food processor and blitz until the mixture is like breadcrumbs. Add the grated carrot and blend to form a pastry ball. On a floured surface, roll out the pastry and line a loose-bottomed flan tin or shallow tart case. Cover and chill for at least 20 minutes in the fridge.

To make the filling, heat the oil in a pan, add the onions and cook over a low heat for about 15–20 minutes. Stir in the sugar and continue to cook until beginning to caramelize.

Spread the grated beetroot in the empty pastry case and cover with the onions. In a bowl, whisk together the eggs, milk and thyme leaves, season and pour over the onions and beetroot. Sprinkle the crumbled feta on top of the mixture.

Place in the oven, and cook for 15 minues, then reduce the temperature to 170°C (gas mark 3) and cook for a further 40 minutes, or until the filling is set, lightly risen and golden brown. Rest the flan for a couple of minutes before serving in generous wedges with salad and bread.

WILD MUSHROOM, SPINACH AND CHEDDAR WELLINGTONS

You can use any strong Cheddar for this recipe, but we'd recommend Isle of Mull Cheddar – a very sharp white Cheddar, sometimes with blue veining – if you can find it.

Serves 4

200g mixed wild mushrooms
4 tbsp olive oil
25 ml (1 dram) The Famous Grouse
2 garlic cloves, crushed
400 g spinach
Pinch of freshly grated nutmeg
Flour, for dusting

500 g ready-made puff pastry
140 g Cheddar, grated
50 g walnut pieces
1 medium egg, beaten
Salt and freshly ground black pepper
Steamed sprouting broccoli, to serve

Preheat oven to 220°C (gas mark 7). Wipe mushrooms clean and slice any large ones in half. Heat half the oil in a large frying pan and sauté the mushrooms for 3–4 minutes until golden and cooked. Remove the pan from the heat and stir in the whisky, then remove the mushrooms from the pan to a bowl.

Next, place the pan back over a medium heat and add the remaining oil. Fry the garlic for a moment, add the spinach and cook for 2–3 minutes over a high heat until wilted. Season with salt, pepper and nutmeg, then drain the spinach through a sieve to remove excess water.

Lightly flour a surface and roll the pastry out to 5 mm thick. Using a saucer and a larger sized plate, cut out 4 circles about 10 cm wide for the bottoms and 4 circles about 15 cm wide for the tops. Use the trimmings if you need to: layer them on top of each other and re-roll; don't squash them up or the pastry won't rise.

Place the 4 smaller circles on a baking sheet and top each with a quarter of the mushroom mixture and a quarter of the spinach mixture. Sprinkle each with a quarter of the Cheddar and a quarter of the walnut pieces. Brush the border to each circle with egg, then gently stretch the larger circle over the filling, trying not to trap any air. Seal the edges with a fork and brush each generously with the beaten egg. Bake for 40 minutes until the pastry is golden and well risen, then leave to cool for a few minutes before serving with steamed sprouting broccoli.

KEEPING IT IN THE FAMILY

Many whiskies carry a proud family name. But just because The Famous Grouse does not have a family name doesn't mean that a family isn't involved.

Meet the Gloag family, creators of The Famous Grouse, and seventh-generation Emma Gloag, who is still involved with the brand created by her forefathers.

It was in 1896 that Perthshire grocer and wine merchant Matthew Gloag first created his whisky. Unconventional from the start, he named his whisky after an iconic Scottish bird rather than himself. It became 'Famous' in 1905 and remained under direct family control until 1970.

Male members of the family were traditionally named Matthew. To this day, the signature of the sixth-generation Matthew Gloag remains embossed into the glass of every bottle. Currently the family name is carried by Emma Gloag, who maintains an active contact with the brand.

The link lives on in Perth, where the company's original HQ, formerly known as Bordeaux House (but now long outgrown by worldwide demand) is today The Bothy. Appropriately enough, it's a restaurant, with a bar (The Famous Grouse) and a private dining room known as The Matthew Gloag Room.

DESSERTS

APPLE TARTE TATIN WITH WHISKY ICE CREAM

A buttery, sweet and rich classic apple dessert that is delicious
served with The Famous Grouse ice cream.

Serves 6

For the whisky ice cream	For the apple tarte tatin
500 ml double cream	100 g sugar
2 vanilla pods	5 eating apples, peeled, cored
70 g caster sugar	and halved
3 egg yolks	100 g butter
50 ml (2 drams) The Famous Grouse	500 g ready-made puff pastry

To make the ice cream, place the cream into a saucepan over a low heat. Halve
the vanilla pods lengthways and scrape out and reserve the seeds. Add the
vanilla pods to the cream and bring to a boil, then add the sugar and stir until
the sugar has dissolved. Meanwhile, whisk the egg yolks in a large bowl, then
slowly whisk in the hot cream mixture.

Pour the mixture through a fine sieve into another bowl and whisk in the
vanilla seeds. Allow to cool, stir in the whisky and either churn in an ice cream
maker until frozen or pour the mixture into a freezer-proof container and
freeze for 2–3 hours, or until set.

To make the tarte tatin, preheat the oven to 190°C (gas mark 5). Put the sugar
and 50 ml water into an ovenproof dish, approx 20 cm in diameter. Place over
a high heat, bring to a boil, then simmer until it turns a light caramel colour.
Carefully add the apples to the pan and cook for about 5 minutes, stirring and
turning them occasionally, until they start to soften. Add the butter and stir.
Remove from the heat then lay the pastry over the top of the dish, tucking it
right into the edges (use a wooden spoon, as the apple mixture will be hot).

Bake for about 25–30 minutes, or until golden, with caramel bubbling up from
the sides. Turn out onto a serving plate and serve hot with whisky ice cream.

THE FAMOUS GROUSE
CHRISTMAS STRUDEL

This is a nice seasonal dish and great warmer for those winter nights.

Serves 4 (makes 2 strudels)

2 eating apples (preferably Cox's), peeled, cored and diced
2 ripe pears, peeled, cored and diced
225 g mincemeat
50 ml (2 drams) The Famous Grouse
Flour, for dusting
1 packet filo pastry (6 large sheets)
50 g butter, melted
2 tsp icing sugar
1 tsp cinnamon
200 g crème fraîche, to serve

Preheat the oven to 200°C (gas mark 6). In a bowl, mix together the apple, pears and mincemeat, stir in the whisky and set aside for 30 minutes.

Place a sheet of filo pastry lengthways on a lightly floured surface and brush with melted butter. Place another sheet on top, brush with melted butter again and top with a third sheet. Spoon half the filling onto the pastry along the edge nearest you, about 2.5 cm from the edge. Roll the filling up in the pastry, tucking the ends in as you go. Place the strudel onto a greased baking sheet. Repeat with the remaining filo pastry sheets and filling.

Brush the outside of the strudels with melted butter and bake in the preheated oven for about 15–20 minutes until golden.

Place on a serving plate and dust with icing sugar and cinnamon. Serve with crème fraîche.

ASSIETTE OF APPLE

Hot apple crumble and apple syllabub served with a quenelle of whisky-scented apple and cinnamon ice cream.

Serves 6

For the apple mixture
50 g butter
800 g cooked apples, peeled, cored
and quartered
2 tsp ground cinnamon
50 g raisins
2 tbsp caster sugar

**For the apple and cinnamon ice
cream (¾ litre mix)**
¼ quantity apple mixture
500 ml double cream
2 vanilla pods
70 g sugar
3 egg yolks
50 ml (2 drams) The Famous Grouse
1 tsp ground cinnamon

For the crumble
½ quantity apple mixture
150 g plain flour, sieved
85 g sugar
100 g butter, cubed
Pinch of salt

For the apple syllabub
¼ quantity apple mixture
1 meringue shell, broken
100 ml whipping cream, whipped to
soft peaks
Cocoa powder, sifted

To serve
3 shortbread biscuits
Icing sugar, sifted

To make the apple mixture, melt the butter in a pan, add the apples, cinnamon, raisins and sugar and cook for about 20 minutes over a low heat until softened. Set aside to cool.

To make the ice cream, place the cream in a saucepan and start to heat. Halve the vanilla pods lengthways and scrape out the seeds. Add the pods to the cream and bring to the boil, then add the sugar and stir until the sugar has dissolved. Meanwhile, whisk the egg yolks in a large bowl then slowly whisk in the hot cream mixture.

Pour the mixture through a fine sieve into another bowl and whisk in the vanilla seeds. Allow to cool, stir in the whisky, ground cinnamon and apple mixture and either churn in an ice-cream maker until frozen or pour the mixture into a freezer-proof container and freeze for 2–3 hours, or until set.

To make the crumble, preheat the oven to 180°C (gas mark 4). Put half the quantity of apple mix into the bottom of 6 ramekin dishes. Put the sieved flour, sugar, butter and a pinch of salt into a bowl and work through your fingers until the mixture resembles coarse breadcrumbs. Scatter this crumble topping on top of the apple mix lightly (do not pat down) and bake in the oven for 15–20 minutes.

To make the syllabub, spoon ¼ of the apple mixture into 6 shot glasses and sprinkle the crushed meringue on top, then cover each with softly whipped cream dust with cocoa powder. Refrigerate until ready to serve.

To serve, place a shot glass of syllabub off centre on each plate, a ramekin of crumble next to it, and then sprinkle some crushed shortbread onto the plate and top with a generous scoop of ice cream. Dust each plate with icing sugar and serve.

CRÈME BRÛLÉE WITH CINNAMON-SCENTED WHISKY ICE CREAM

Serves 8

For the cinnamon-scented whisky ice cream
500 ml double cream
2 vanilla pods
70 g caster sugar
1 tsp ground cinnamon
3 egg yolks
50 ml (2 drams) The Famous Grouse
2 shortbread biscuits

For the crème brûlée
500 ml double cream
1 vanilla pod
100 g caster sugar (plus an extra 6 tsp for the topping)
6 egg yolks
25 ml (1 dram) The Famous Grouse

To make the ice cream, place the cream in a saucepan and start to heat. Halve the vanilla pods lengthways and scrape out and reserve the seeds. Add the pods to the cream and bring to the boil, then add the sugar and cinnamon and stir until the sugar has dissolved.

Meanwhile, whisk the egg yolks in a large bowl then slowly whisk in the hot cream mixture.

Pour the mixture through a fine sieve into another bowl and whisk in the vanilla seeds. Allow to cool, mix in the whisky and crumbled shortbread biscuits and either churn in an ice-cream maker until frozen or pour the mixture into a freezer-proof container and freeze for 2–3 hours, or until set.

To make the crème brûlée, preheat the oven to 140°C (gas mark 1). Pour the cream into a saucepan. Split the vanilla pod lengthways and scrape the seeds into the cream. Finely chop the empty pod and add to the cream. Bring to a boil, then lower the heat and simmer gently for 5 minutes.

Beat the sugar and egg yolks together in a large heatproof bowl until pale and creamy. Bring the cream back to boiling point and pour it over the egg mixture, whisking all the time until thickened (this indicates that the eggs have begun to cook slightly). Strain through a fine sieve into a large jug, stir in the whisky then pour into 6 ramekins until about two-thirds full.

Place the ramekins in a large roasting tray and pour in enough hot water to come halfway up their sides. Place on the centre shelf of the oven and bake for about 30 minutes, or until the custards are just set and are still a bit wobbly in the middle. Remove from the water and cool to room temperature, then store in the fridge until ready to serve.

When ready to serve, sprinkle 1 level teaspoon of caster sugar evenly over the surface of each crème brûlée, then caramelize under the grill or using a mini blowtorch. Leave to cool for a couple of minutes before serving. Serve each crème brûlée with a generous scoop of whisky ice cream.

SCOTTISH FRUIT JELLIES

Fresh summer berries are set in The Snow Grouse and Champagne
jelly and served with a duo of passion fruit coulis and tuile biscuit.

Serves 6

For the jelly
200 g fresh raspberries
200 g fresh strawberries
200 g fresh blackberries
200 g fresh redcurrants
25 g fresh mint
100 g caster sugar
½ bottle of Champagne or
sparkling wine
100 ml (4 drams) The Snow Grouse
3 leaves of gelatine

For the passion fruit coulis
8 ripe passion fruit
1 tbsp caster sugar

For the tuile biscuits
50 g butter
50 g icing sugar
1 medium egg, beaten
50 g plain flour

Divide the raspberries, strawberries, blackberries, redcurrants and mint evenly between 6 ramekin dishes. Put the gelatine leaves into a bowl and cover with cold water. Leave to soak for at least 5 minutes.

Put the sugar, Champagne and The Snow Grouse in a pan over a low heat until the sugar has dissolved. Remove the gelatine from the soaking water, squeeze out any excess water and then add to the Champagne mixture and stir to dissolve. Pour the mixture over the berries, filling the ramekins, and place in the fridge to set for at least 2 hours.

Make the passion fruit coulis while the jellies are setting. Halve each passion fruit and scrape the pulp and seeds into a small saucepan. Stir in the sugar and bring to a boil. Simmer for a minute or so, stirring, then remove from the heat and allow to cool.

To make the tuile biscuits, preheat the oven to 200°C (gas mark 6). Place the butter and icing sugar in a bowl and beat together until light and fluffy. Beat in the egg and then gently fold in the flour.

Line 2 baking sheets with greaseproof paper. Place 1–2 teaspoons of the mixture on a baking sheet and spread it thinly to make a round 6–8cm in diameter. Make another 1 or 2 rounds on the sheet. Bake for 5–8 minutes, or until they start to turn a pale golden colour.

Remove the baking sheet from the oven and, working quickly, slide a metal palette knife under the tuile biscuits to release them, then drape them over a rolling pin, so that they cool into a curved shape.

Repeat the baking and shaping process with the remaining mixture (you should have 12 tuile biscuits when you finish).

To serve, carefully immerse the ramekins one at a time in a bowl of very hot water, then turn out onto serving plates. Serve with a couple of tuile biscuits and a generous swirl of passion fruit coulis.

800 YEARS STRONG

It's not every day that your home town celebrates 800 years of history. So naturally, The Famous Grouse felt they had to mark the 800 years since King William the Lion of Scotland handed Perth its Charter as a Royal Burgh.

The result is the striking Grouse Statue on the centre of the roundabout at Broxden, just outside the city itself, a lasting legacy for the people of Perth from one of its leading companies.

The dramatic sculpture was created by leading sculptor Ruaraig Maciver from Beltane Studios in Peebles and all the costs of construction and installation were paid for by The Famous Grouse.

Made from an open framework of galvanized steel, The Grouse sculpture is approximately 2,500 times the weight of a real red grouse, and 37 times its height. Standing proud at an impressive 15 m (49 ft) tall (including the 9 m/29 ft column) and weighing 1.5 tonnes, the sculpture is already established as one of the most striking public artworks in Scotland.

That's one big bird!

DRINKS

lime

THE FAMOUS GROUSE

Scotland's favourite whisky creates a passion for food
and whisky. It is one of the world's great drinks, smooth
and easy to enjoy. The dark chocolate, mature orange
notes offer a match to most meat dishes and seafood.
It is often referred to as the Scottish wine!

THE FAMOUS COBBLER

Berries are muddled together with orange segments, raspberry liqueur, port and The Famous Grouse. This cocktail is great served at a party or as a digestif.

37.7 ml (1½ drams) The Famous Grouse
37.5 ml port
12.5 ml raspberry liqueur
½ orange, cut into chunks
4 raspberries, plus 1 or 2 extra to decorate
3 blackberries, plus 1 or 2 extra to decorate

Set aside a few berries as a decoration, then place all remaining ingredients into a cocktail shaker and muddle together. Add ice and shake. Fill a tall glass with ice and strain over the cocktail ingredients. Decorate with the reserved berries.

HONEY & MARMALADE SOUR

The Famous Grouse is shaken with fresh lemon and marmalade, whose sharpness is soothed with clear honey. This goes well with Trout with an Orange and Fennel Crust (page 81).

50 ml (2 drams) The Famous Grouse
25 ml freshly squeezed lemon juice
1 teaspoon clear honey
1 teaspoon marmalade
Orange zest, to decorate

Place all the ingredients except the orange zest into a cocktail shaker, add ice, shake and strain into a chilled cocktail glass. Decorate with orange zest.

THE GINGER GROUSE

A simple and refreshing mix of The Famous Grouse and fresh lime
served over ice and sparkled with fiery ginger beer. This is a simple
drink to be enjoyed on any occasion.

1 fresh lime wedge
25 ml (1 dram) The Famous Grouse
Ginger beer

Fill a tall glass with ice, squeeze over a lime wedge, add The Famous Grouse
and top with fiery ginger beer.

THE FAMOUS MILK PUNCH

A creamy and luxurious combination of The Famous Grouse,
cream, white chocolate liqueur and vanilla syrup. The ultimate
after-dinner cocktail.

25 ml (1 dram) The Famous Grouse
50 ml single cream
12.5 ml white chocolate liqueur
2 tsp vanilla syrup
Grated chocolate, to decorate

Place all the ingredients except the grated chocolate into a cocktail shaker, add
ice, shake and strain into a cocktail glass. Decorate with grated chocolate.

THE LABEL

By the end of the nineteenth century the market for blended whiskies had begun to take off. Cognac supplies had dwindled following the devastation of French vineyards by the phylloxera blight, and Scotland had become fashionable thanks to the poems and novels of Sir Walter Scott and royal patronage from Queen Victoria and Prince Albert. Blended whiskies were accessible, affordable and stylish.

Gloags of Perth had seen their wine and spirit business grow steadily, and in 1896 Matthew Gloag decided that the firm needed its own brand. His daughter Philippa, an accomplished amateur artist, drew the red grouse that graced the label of the 'Grouse Brand' – a name chosen to appeal to the sporting fraternity who came to the Highlands of Scotland for hunting, shooting and fishing.

Soon the brand was famous and, in 1905, the name was changed to reflect this. Little else changed until 1984 when a Royal Warrant was proudly added. The packaging was subtly updated in 2004 and again in 2010.

The grouse still features, of course, but did you know you can order your own personalised bottle online at www.thefamousegrouse.com. You can be famous too!

THE BLACK GROUSE

When it comes to 'fusion' The Black Grouse excels. Smoky but smooth, it is the traditional match for smoked meat or vegetables, and rich cheese also complements it perfectly. This blend of flavours offers an interesting contrast, too: try it diluted with water with rich vanilla fudge – sublime!

THE SMOKY SOUR

A peaty twist on the classic Whiskey Sour, this combines the sweet smoky flavour of The Black Grouse with fresh lemon and sugar syrup. It goes particularly well with Arbroath Smokie Tarts (page 76).

50 ml (2 drams) The Black Grouse
25 ml freshly squeezed lemon juice
12.5 ml sugar syrup

Place all the ingredients into a cocktail shaker, add ice and shake. Place some ice cubes into a short glass and strain over the cocktail.

BAD APPLE BUCK

The Black Grouse marries beautifully with pressed apple juice, fresh lime and ginger beer. Try this cocktail with Apple Tarte Tatin (page 102).

1 fresh lime wedge
25 ml (1 dram) The Black Grouse
50 ml pressed apple juice
Ginger beer

Add ice to a tall glass and squeeze over the lime wedge. Add The Black Grouse and pressed apple juice and top with ginger beer.

PINEAPPLE & MINT BLOSSOM

Fresh pineapple chunks are muddled with The Black Grouse,
sugar syrup and fresh mint and served in a cocktail glass
to make a great aperitif.

50 ml (2 drams) The Black Grouse
12.5 ml sugar syrup
5 pineapple chunks
5 fresh mint leaves

Place all the ingredients into a cocktail shaker and muddle together, then add
ice and shake. Strain into a chilled cocktail glass.

THE BLACK & BLACK

The smoky character of The Black Grouse combined with freshly
squeezed orange juice and topped with cola makes a simple drink
to be enjoyed on any occasion.

25 ml (1 dram) The Black Grouse
1 generous wedge of orange
Cola

Place some ice cubes into tall glass and squeeze over the orange wedge.
Pour over The Black Grouse and top up with cola.

SAVING THE BLACK GROUSE

Just as The Famous Grouse has a relative, The Black Grouse (a peatier style), so the red grouse has a larger relation, also known as the black grouse.

A strikingly handsome bird with attractive blue-black plumage, a white stripe on the wing and a distinctive red 'eyebrow', the Black Grouse is sadly under threat in the UK. Conservation work to protect its habitat in Scotland is thought particularly important for the species.

The Famous Grouse is supporting the RSPB's research and conservation programme and has already raised over £200,000 to help save this magnificent bird from extinction.

The RSPB runs mini safaris through Corrimony Nature Reserve where – if you're lucky – you'll catch a glimpse of the 'lek' or mating display. But don't despair if you don't see a thing, as evening safaris end with a whisky tasting and every adult visitor takes home their own Black Grouse.

In a miniature bottle, that is!

THE NAKED GROUSE

The Naked Grouse carries the blueprint of The Famous Grouse, the DNA of this famous Scotch resulting in ultra-smoothness, highlighting the importance of the sherry casks. Buttery and delightfully sherried, it works well with a wide range of foods and will temper the zest of the sharpest fruit compote. There is something of the exotic in this whisky, and it is equally at home with game dishes and The Famous Grouse Christmas Strudel (page 103).

THE ROB ROY

The Naked Grouse slowly stirred until chilled with Angostura bitters and sweet vermouth, then decorated with lemon zest and a cherry. This cocktail can be enjoyed before or after dinner.

50 ml (2 drams) The Naked Grouse
25 ml sweet vermouth
2 dashes Angostura bitters
Lemon zest, to decorate
1 cocktail cherry, to decorate

Place ice into a cocktail shaker, add The Naked Grouse, sweet vermouth and Angostura bitters and stir for 20 seconds. Strain into a chilled cocktail glass and decorate with lemon zest and a cocktail cherry.

NAKED OLD FASHIONED

A true gentleman's cocktail, and a great after-dinner drink, in which The Naked Grouse, Angostura bitters and sugar are all stirred together with ice and decorated with orange zest.

2 tsp sugar syrup
2 dashes Angostura bitters
50 ml (2 drams) The Naked Grouse
Orange zest, to decorate

Add the sugar and bitters to a large whisky glass, stir together, add 25 ml The Naked Grouse and half fill the glass with ice. Stir for 10 seconds, then fill the glass with ice and add the last 25 ml of The Naked Grouse. Stir for a further 10 seconds, then decorate with orange zest.

BLOOD & SAND

Named after the 1922 movie of the same name, this cocktail mixes
The Naked Grouse with cherry liqueur, sweet vermouth and freshly
squeezed orange juice. A great match for Duck à la Grouse (pages 56–7).

25 ml (1 dram) The Naked Grouse
25 ml sweet vermouth
25 ml freshly squeezed orange juice
25 ml cherry liqueur
1 cocktail cherry, to decorate

Place all the ingredients except the cocktail cherry into a cocktail shaker, add ice,
shake and strain into a chilled cocktail glass. Decorate with the cherry.

CAT AND MOUSE

Not many cats have their own statue. Even fewer make it into the Guinness Book of Records as World Mousing Champion.

But, then, very few cats can claim to have caught 28,899 mice! That's the proud record of the late and sadly lamented Towser, distillery cat at the Glenturret distillery. In 24 years dedicated service from 1963 until her death in 1987, this long-haired tortoiseshell female trapped an average of three mice a day.

The rumour is that she was partial to a tiny wee dram of whisky in her night-time milk but, whatever her secret, she took it to the grave. Today Dylan and Brooke have taken over her basket, and even have their own private entrance to the still house.

Perhaps the distillery is a tidier place these days, as Towser's record doesn't seem in any danger. Or perhaps the mice have just learned to stay away.

THE SNOW GROUSE

Think vanilla and coconut ice cream. This is a different sensory experience. Served 'seriously chilled', The Snow Grouse becomes gloopy (thicker) and reveals an elegant sweetness. It can cut through oily fish and complements perfectly any dessert. What better way to toast the evening than to raise a glass of The Snow Grouse, served straight from the freezer!

THE VANILLA SODA

This cocktail combines The Snow Grouse with fresh lime and vanilla syrup and is lengthened with lemon soda. It makes a good particularly good match with mackerel.

25 ml (1 dram) The Snow Grouse
2 tsp vanilla syrup
2 fresh lime wedges
Soda water

Fill a tall glass with ice, squeeze over the lime wedges, add The Snow Grouse and vanilla syrup, top with soda water and stir gently.

THE SNOW JULEP

Vanilla syrup is infused with fresh mint and The Snow Grouse and then churned with crushed ice. This cocktail goes well with Scottish Fruit Jellies (page 108–9)

50 ml (2 drams) The Snow Grouse
2 tsp vanilla syrup
8 fresh mint leaves
Crushed ice
1 fresh mint leaf, to serve

Place The Snow Grouse, vanilla syrup and mint leaves into a short glass and gently muddle together. Add some crushed ice to the glass and stir, then top up with more crushed ice and decorate with the fresh mint sprig.

Acknowledgements

Ian Buxton, for the introductory text (pages 9–47) and feature pages throughout the book.

Steven Craik, Executive Head Chef, The Famous Grouse Experience

Andy Gemmell, Mixologist, Mixxit